IT'S ABOUT TIME – UNDERSTANDING CHINA'S STRATEGIC PATIENCE

> The developing coherence of Asian regional thinking is reflected in a disposition to consider problems and loyalties in regional terms, and to evolve regional approaches to development needs and to the evolution of a new world order.[1]

— Richard Nixon

Richard Nixon understood in 1967 that Asian thinking was different, and that Asia, specifically China, was evolving towards great world relevance. The future President Nixon even illustrated where the United States strategic planners and thinkers lacked a specific understanding of the Asian mind.[2] China was becoming a force to be reckoned with, perhaps even in a future conflict. As China was seen by the United States as a rising power to be dealt with in the future, strategists and leaders in the United States would need to apply a better understanding of how their potential adversary may think. Hence, given today's tenuous relationship between the United States and China, the applicability and relevance of Western (American) thinkers and strategists to understand Asian thought is as relevant as ever. Of the many differences between the United States and China, a large and often overlooked difference is the viewpoint of how each nation interprets and applies the concept of time.

This paper will explore the applicability of time as a critical factor in the elements of national power, specifically the differences in how the concept of time is applied by Eastern and Western powers. A basic definition of time will be presented illustrating theories accepted by both the United States and Chinese. Judeo Christian time versus Taoist thoughts of time will be presented and will be used to illustrate differences on a cultural level, and how time applies to the diplomatic, information, military and economic arenas, and examine if or how time is a critical aspect of each element of national power. While analyzing the military element of power, a specific question for exploration is, does time serve as a warfare domain such as the current domains of land, air, maritime, space and cyber?

This paper will conclude with a discussion of the potential for future conflict between China and the United States and an analysis of how time, in the Chinese national strategy, is evident in today's interaction with the United States.

Time: A Scientific Analysis

The question, "what is time?" is both simple and incredibly complex. Some of the most well known works in the area of astrophysics illustrate scientific viewpoints of time, which are widely accepted in both Eastern and Western scholarly circles. Eastern and Western scholars typically agree on the first post-Newtonian theory of time-space in Albert Einstein's Theory of Relativity and his concept of Physical Time.[3] If science defines a common viewpoint held by both Eastern and Western scholars, what exists between Eastern and Western societies as a significant fundamental difference in the two interpretations of the concept of time, is culture. The scientific analysis of time here is to assist in defining this "time difference" in cultural relativity.

Webster's Dictionary lists fourteen definitions for time, six as a noun – five more as a verb and three as an adjective. Defining Time is difficult – we cannot observe time using our physical senses. We can only observe the physical affects of the passage of time. Our understanding that time "passes" allows us to envision that a future must also exist.[4] At its simplest definition, time is what clocks measure and time's most complex and widely accepted definition draws from scientific basis from the world's most noted scholars and scientists. These scientists, such as Albert Einstein and Stephen

Hawking, made conceptualizing time easier to accept by linking time with space. Time and space are inherently linked together in man's understanding of time.

The Theory of Relativity

In the latter part of the 19th century, physicists were searching for the mysterious thing called ether - the medium they believed existed for light waves to move through.[5] This belief that ether existed made understanding space and time difficult, in Einstein's view, by introducing a medium that caused certain laws of physics to work differently depending on how the observer moved relative to the ether. Einstein's analysis removed the ether entirely and assumed that the laws of physics, including the speed of light, worked the same regardless of how you were moving - exactly as experiments and mathematics of the day showed them to be.

In 1905, Albert Einstein published the theory of special relativity, which explained how to interpret motion between different frames of reference; places that are moving at constant speeds relative to each other. Einstein explained that when two objects are moving at independent constant speeds, emphasizing the relative motion between the two objects, vice making the ether or space, the absolute frame of reference.[6] An example would be if the reader was driving an automobile and another motorist was moving in a different automobile, and they want to compare observations. All that matters is how fast the reader and the other motorist were moving with respect to each other. Special relativity includes only the special case where the motion is in a straight line and at a constant speed. As soon as one accelerates or turns - or does anything that changes the nature of the motion in any way - special relativity ceases to apply. That's where Einstein's general theory of relativity comes in, because it can explain the general case of any sort of motion. Einstein's theory was based on two key principles:

3

1. The principle of relativity: The laws of physics don't change, even for objects moving in constant speed frames of reference.

2. The principle of the speed of light: The speed of light is the same for all observers, regardless of their motion relative to the light source. Physicists write this speed using the symbol c.

The genius of Einstein's discoveries is that he looked at the experiments and assumed the findings were true. This was the exact opposite of what other physicists of Einstein's era were doing. Instead of assuming the theory was correct and that the experiments failed, he assumed that the experiments were correct and the theory had failed. Einstein's theory of special relativity created a fundamental link between space and time. The universe can be viewed as having three space dimensions - up/down, left/right, forward/backward - and one time dimension.[7] This four-dimensional space is referred to as the space-time continuum and proves critical in understanding the relational difference in time orientation due to what Einstein proved – it's all about one's viewpoint relative to another observer.[8]

<u>Unifying Space and Time</u>

Stephen W Hawking wrote, "Through [a] wormhole, the scientist can see himself as he was one minute ago. But what if our scientist uses the wormhole to shoot his earlier self? He's now dead. So who fired the shot?[9] This quote describes a hypothetical scenario that illustrates the great complexity of time and evokes thought on the relationship of past, present and future. Time has been a major subject of religion, philosophy, and science, but creating a common definition for time applicable to all fields of study has eluded scholars. Most would agree that time is a concept that humans use to place events in sequence one after the other, to compare how long an event lasts, and to tell when an event occurs. One could argue that time is a concept created by man to keep track of things to order and categorize when they happen.[10]

To the Western Judeo-Christian thinker, time is a complex series of events, which flow in one direction from starting point A to end point B. Hence, time is a linear flow through an established list of events.[11] To the Chinese Taoist, time is a cycle of day and night, where the day must follow the night and the night must be preceded by the day. Thus, the Taoist's time is a circle or a cycle of things that occur naturally and in balance with each other. This illustration of circular time is an analogy applied by a Western thinker's understanding of Eastern time and not what a Taoist actually believes. This relativity of time's perceived directional vector creates the basis for understanding a culture's time orientation.

Chronemics and Time-Orientation

Different cultures have different attitudes toward time – or different "time orientations."[12] There is no more powerful, pervasive influence on how individuals think and cultures interact than our different perspectives on time-the way we learn how we mentally partition time into past, present and future.[13] The way an individual perceives time and the role time plays in their lives is a learned perspective. Every child learns a time perspective that is appropriate to the values and needs of his society.[14] This societal importance of time greatly affects verbal and non-verbal communication. Communication is important and can directly influence and affect communication of diplomacy, negotiation, and conflict resolution. Non-verbal communication especially is important because one will tend to look for non-verbal cues when the verbal message becomes unclear or ambiguous.

Polychronic Time Orientation

The term polychronic can be used to describe a culture where multiple activities are undertaken at the same time. Time scheduling is very fluid, as the culture is focused more on relationships than "clock watching". These cultures are generally older, "traditional" cultures, such as China. Polychronic cultures have a long-term orientation, emphasizing persistence, thrift, flexibility, and the importance and applicability of past events and decisions.[15] These cultures are highly contextual and consider non-verbal communication as equally important as verbal communication. Polychronic cultures emphasize the importance and applicability of past events and decisions. This includes what short-term oriented cultures such as the United States would consider distant past. For the Chinese, the opium wars of the nineteenth century and the Boxer Rebellion are still relevant to, and come up in the discussion of contemporary issues.[16] Consider this point as a Western thinker, as modern-day leaders in the United States find relevance in the conduct of World War I and apply it to today's issues. Polychronic time orientation's "wheel of time" is also evident in religious beliefs and ancient cultures or religions such as Incan, Mayan, Greek, Hindu, Buddhist, Jainist, Taoist and Native American tribes have a concept of a wheel.[17] These cultures and/or religions view time as a cycle consisting of repeated ages that happen to every being in the universe between birth and extinction.

Monochronic Time Orientation

In contrast to polychronic time orientation, monochronic cultures tend to do one thing at a time with emphasis placed on executing a plan. Time keeping and adherence to schedule are important, as is expeditious completion of the current task in order to move on to the next. This is indicative of "modern" cultures such as the United States.

These cultures have a short-term orientation and are very present and future-focused, emphasizing efficiency, promptness, and adherence to plans.[18] Organization, planning and goal achievement are the cornerstones of success. The expression "time is money" is popular in US culture, where time is perceived as a commodity that can be saved, spent, and wasted. Time is directly tied to monetary value. Businesses constantly strive to complete tasks "more efficiently". This is often defined as: in less time and at less cost. Monochronic cultures are low context and place less emphasis on non-verbal communication.

Time in a monochronic society is also based upon the religion for which the society was founded. The United States follows a traditional Judeo-Christian time orientation. That is, God created the world at a specific time in history and that the world will end at a certain time at which point those individual's souls will be judged by their creator. Thus, this time line is made up of a present that became past and a future that will flow from present to past as defined by God's will. A Judeo-Christian value system, based on the Bible or Torah, has been the prevalent value system in the United States. Judeo-Christian time orientation portrays time as a line, beginning with the act of God creating the heaven and Earth. Hence, this linear time orientation is best stated as the world was created by God at a specific time and will end at a specific time determined by God.[19]

Rapid Dominance and Strategic Patience

To effect the strategic environment in the 21st century requires an understanding of polychronic, monochronic and cultural aspects of time and how each are perceived by Eastern and Western military strategists. Time is a marker of value. Tactically, this value can be best described militarily as speed and tempo. The gaining or losing of time and effectiveness relative to one's continued mobility or developing position, especially with respect to the number of moves required to gain a specific objective is of greatest value. Speed and tempo may be of utmost importance at the operational and tactical levels of war, but there may be a different element of patience at the strategic level that is not well understood nor practiced in the West.

The United States approach to warfare is to employ a concept of rapid dominance. This is a military doctrine based on the use of overwhelming power, dominant battlefield situational awareness, dominant maneuvers, and disproportionate displays of force to paralyze an adversary's perception of the battlefield and destroy its will to fight.[20] This style of warfare's goal is to seize control of a warfare domain and saturate an adversary's perception and understanding of events hence rendering the enemy incapable of resistance. This style of warfare mirrors the monochronic emphasis on expeditious completion of a task in order to move on to the next task.

In Chinese polychronic thought, influenced by Taoism, the sum of all things must remain in balance.[21] Time must be balanced and optimal for action, including exercising strategic patience to ensure the time is right for action. In an attempt to explain the differences between Chinese and Western thought, the French Sinologist, Francois Jullien struggled with the inability to easily translate the Chinese word "Shi".[22] It is no coincidence that Jullien found it difficult to translate this single word, which in essence indicates there is a facet of Eastern thought that, does not occur in the West. It is also important to note there is no word for "time" in classical Chinese language that directly conveys the meaning of the Western word "time".

Jullien describes *shi* as a collection of great energy that possesses great power if used properly, like the arrow resting on a coiled crossbow. The weapon of analogy is important; a crossbow fires an arrow at a flatter trajectory with much greater speed than a reflex bow. The crossbow's speed and trajectory make the arrow unseen to the naked eye. Hence, the arrow fired from the crossbow will be enroute to its target long before the prey ever sees it. *Shi* is the energy of a nation, an army or the activity used at the optimal moment in the cycle of time by a skilled leader.[23] In short, the leader must expend its *shi* in a balance between the Yin (strength) of the army and the Yang (weakness) of the foe.

To best comprehend the Eastern polychronic approach, one must be aware of the perspective of time in Sun Tzu's work, the 36 Ancient Chinese Strategems and the concept of shi. Sun Tzu was an acclaimed Chinese strategist who lived in the 5th Century before Christ's Existence (BCE). Sun Tzu's *The Art of War* has remained a principle guiding document for Chinese strategy and warfare for over 2500 years.[24] Sun Tzu was almost certainly a follower of Taoism, founded by Lao-Tzu. Taoism and Western belief are vastly different, particularly in the simple yet highly indefinable concept of time.[25] Both Eastern and Western doctrines stress destruction of the enemy's will rather than merely of his physical forces. The most prevalent strategy in use by the Chinese is the concept of winning without fighting. Strategically, patience, or the acceptance of protraction is a Taoist view and something less prevalent in Western strategy.[26] Thus, the application of rapid dominance employed by the United States may not be an appropriate and effective way to combat Eastern Shi.

The Thirty-Six Ancient Stratagems

The *Thirty-Six Ancient Stratagems* was a Chinese essay from 500 BCE used to illustrate a series of stratagems used in politics, war, as well as in diplomacy and economic interaction, often through unseen, or deceptive means.[27] The stratagems were divided into six groups that discussed stratagems for use in a superior position, confrontation, attack, confused situations, gaining ground and for desperate situations. In today's high-technology internet-centric society, the thirty-six ancient stratagems of China would appear to be outdated. However, a look at a stratagem from each category will illustrate how ancient concepts remain applicable in today's modern, interconnected world and how a nation like China employs these stratagems in their elements of national power.

China's Economic War on the United States

Ancient Stratagem Seventeen states, "Steal the firewood from under the pot." This means that when faced with an enemy too powerful to engage directly you must first weaken him by undermining his foundation and attacking his source of power.[28] The Ancient Stratagems are "alive and well" and in practice today – most notably in the areas of economic and informational elements of Chinese national power.

The most significant interaction between the United States and China is the economic tie between the two nations. In economic terms, the two countries may appear to be friendly toward one another, each supporting each the other's economy through trade, manufacturing and a free market. Financial experts have cited that the Chinese have been waging war with the West for the past ten years.[29]

If one goes back further and considers the near-destruction of the United States steel industry in the 1970s, the era of Chinese eco-war is much more developed and in keeping with the People's Liberation Army (PLA) doctrine of Unrestricted Warfare published in 1999.[30] Over the past forty years, the United States has become a consumer more than a producer of once staple products such as steel and is now less competitive in the world economy with the two largest steel producers in the world, Japan and China, combining to export six times more steel than the United States.[31] A short-view analysis may show that the United States lost on the free market due to an inability to compete by manufacturing steel with aged blast furnace technology, but was the near-death of United States steel industry economic mismanagement by the Americans, or a long-term Chinese strategic effort to thwart a sleeping giant's capability for large-scale kinetic war? The United States failed to see China's economic long-term intentions until its steel industry was all but gone, an example of a short-sighted monochronic time orientation and inability to act for the long term and without knowledge of the near past.

In addition to a dwindling industrial base, needed for economic growth and war sustainment, the United States also has a large national debt in excess of four trillion dollars owned by foreign nations, including China. China's United States investments suggest China's intent to integrate Sino-American economies further to weaken the United States.[32] Official Chinese activity consistent with Economic Warfare demonstrates an endorsement of the Unrestricted Warfare doctrine. In August 2011 The People's Daily, China's leading newspaper, stated it was time for Beijing to consider using its "financial weapon" against the United States.[33] The Communist Party's flagship publication suggested that the Chinese government directly link its purchases of US Treasury debt to Taiwan arms sales and require ratings agencies to downgrade the United States in order to increase American interest payments to China. The paper also suggests China should launch limited trade sanctions against those US states doing business with China whose Congressional representatives support arms sales to Taiwan. "China-US relations will always be constrained by these people and will continue along a roller coaster pattern if China does not beat them until they feel the pain," the paper said. The context of this article is based largely on a recent United States decision to sell advanced fighter aircraft technology to the Taiwanese.[34] The official Chinese Xinhua News Agency issued a recent verbal attack on the United States calling for international supervision over Washington's printing of dollars and suggested consideration of a new international reserve currency to replace the United States dollar "to avert a catastrophe caused by any single country." Skeptics will properly point out that the Chinese are somewhat trapped into buying and holding US Treasury bonds. There is no other economic market deep enough or large enough to accommodate Chinese reserve holdings.[35]

The 21st Century will continue China's quiet emergence as a challenger to the United States military and economic hegemony. China's passive aggression toward the United States suggests it is employing a strategy to subjugate the United States without a need for military confrontation. Sun Tzu states the "best victory is when the opponent surrenders of its own accord before there are any actual hostilities." Hence; it is best to win without fighting. Chinese economic investment in United States Treasury Bills and US corporate interests in China make the United States economically dependent on China – a scenario that China has carefully calculated. The United States economy will be weakened again after the Iraq and Afghanistan wars, when Americans clamor for a peace dividend and the United States embarks on a military drawdown.[36]

Scholars speculate the Chinese Gross Domestic Product (GDP) figure will pass that of the United States by 2016, the leading GDP since the 1890s.[37] Economists and scholars believe that China and the United States could continue down an inevitable path to war based largely on economic reasons.[38]

The Art of Diplomacy with China

Ancient Stratagem Thirty states "Hide your dagger behind a smile." Charm and ingratiate yourself to your enemy. When you have gained his trust, you move against him in secret.[39] Monochronic and polychronic time oriented cultures have interacted throughout history. An American example is the monochronic, Judeo-Christian culture's appearance in North America and its interaction with the polychronic Native American Nations.[40]

The Native American Indians had little use for small elements of time. The cyclical passage of the seasons, marked by the "moons" of the lunar calendar; the years, marked by the passage of "winters"; the division of days and nights into "sleeps": These cycles were sufficient for people who did not know the value of a time clock, "get to work on time," or meet a train-bus-airplane schedule, and for whom, therefore, seconds and minutes and hours were generally useless. Some native peoples in North America used a measure of time they called "a hand," meaning the amount of time it would take the sun to pass from one side to the other of a hand extended at arm's length toward the sun. But this measure was highly variable in a seasonal sense (it also would have varied depending on the size of the observer's hand) and probably was not widely adopted. Because the time-sense of native peoples was so vastly different from

13

that of people who carried timepieces that marked seconds and minutes and hours, European and American explorers had difficulty translating native descriptions of time.[41]

This time-space disconnect between cultures also would create friction between the United States and a Native American Tribe in negotiating settlements, peace treaties and ultimately peaceful coexistence. The monochronic-oriented American approach to dealing with a polychronic culture typically showed little adherence to a long-term strategy of diplomacy and negotiations to deal with the Native Americans. Negotiation with the Indians was typically done through signed treaties and the written word, neither of which had value in the Native American culture.[42] The most common means to the deal with the Native Americans was to advise the Nation of the United States' intent and to then convey a military threat if the Native Americans did not comply. Given this American strategic example from the 19th Century, has American application of power changed dramatically to develop a cohesive long-term strategy with a 21st Century foe?

US Diplomacy with China in the 21st Century will require a long view; toward the future as well as the past in order to be successful. Diplomacy is defined as the art or conduct by government officials of negotiations and other relations between nations or the skill in managing negotiations and handling people so there is little or no ill will between parties. The monochronic-oriented US approach to diplomacy and negotiations is direct, linear and based more on facts and figures than on context. This low context and individualistic-centric culture approaches diplomacy in a lawyerly fashion with arguments, agendas, a mission and an idea of how they will move to exploit the process to their own advantage. A monochronic culture, concerned with

14

time, deadlines and schedules, tends to grow impatient and wants to rush to "close the deal."

Polychronic-oriented Chinese culture approaches diplomatic situations with little importance on time. This culture is more willing to let time tick away if it means they are having a meaningful discussion and are forming strong relationships with the individual(s) with whom they are negotiating. The polychronic culturist will also place tremendous value on the context of the negotiation. Rather than relying solely on verbal or written messages, the high context negotiator operates with a greater emphasis on nonverbal communication. This use of chronemics, or non-verbal communications, is as important as what is said in diplomacy with the Chinese.[43] Slow-moving diplomacy is best suited to the Chinese diplomat who has a long view and an option for protraction and delay. Typically the monochronic American diplomat will sense this delay and either negotiate a settlement or strike a compromise to ensure the appearance of progress is evident to the monochronic democracy's senior leaders wanting to make progress in four to eight years, the typical term of office for senior elected US officials.

Instead of watching the clock, the Chinese prefer discussing broad themes and philosophies before the details of a negotiation are addressed. Above all else, they place far less value on simply reaching agreement for the sake of meeting a deadline. Rather, they place greater value on ensuring the outcome of any agreement "is good and looks good" so that they can preserve face, as is the norm in the polychronic culture as well as a monochronic culture.[44] The Chinese will strive for unilateral or bilateral business and treaty agreements to keep potential partners or adversaries in one on one negotiations vice multilateral negotiations where many parties could unite against

China. In summary, when engaging the Chinese the unspoken word and "how" a diplomat communicates with a Chinese counterpart is as critical as what is said.[45] For Americans, understanding these cultural differences and perspectives on time can greatly improve future negotiations in the international community.

Chinese Information Warfare Aspect of Time-Space Orientation

Ancient Stratagem Twenty Five states, "Replace the beams with rotten timbers." Disrupt the enemy's formations, interfere with their methods of operations, change the rules they are used to following, go contrary to their standard training. In this way one removes the supporting pillar, the common link that makes a group of men an effective fighting force.[46]

Technology has drastically changed the rate at which information can be transmitted. This increase in capability has decreased the time to communicate and influence decisions, commerce and actions around the globe to a matter of seconds. Consider that in the 1700s a message sent from a political leader to his army in the new world could take in excess of a month for a courier to deliver the message. In the 1800s, moving a person that same distance by ship and horse would take weeks. The advent of the aircraft in the 20th Century has shortened this trip to days or hours. Travel by spacecraft turned days and hours of travel into minutes. Today's information environment can move large amounts of information around the world at the speed of light. Cyberspace is the domain where China conducts the most war-like behavior against the United States. The use of regular e-mail services or Internet business links to mask insertions of malicious code or viruses is an example of luring the enemy into a false sense of security. The target of choice by the Chinese has been the servers and networks responsible for Western financial, political and military systems. These activities infiltrate an adversary's network by conducting cyber attacks with malicious code. The Chinese allow and support non-military warriors in attacking other nation's networks. Chinese students or businesses typically execute this proxy-attack cyber strategy inside the Western nation of interest to the Chinese.

The Military Aspect of Time-Space Orientation

Ancient Stratagem Eleven states, "Sacrifice the plum tree in place of the peach." There are circumstances in which you must sacrifice short-term objectives in order to gain the long-term goal. This is the scapegoat strategy whereby someone else suffers the consequences so that the rest do not.[47]

If an understanding of an adversary's cultural beliefs may be used as a tactic by negotiators - Is it possible that the Chinese military understands the US's monochronic short-term orientation, our narrow focus on individual actions and events and how they pertain to a single goal? Are we missing the "bigger picture" that might come into focus with a broader look across a longer period of time? Would the US see multiple actions and events aimed toward a single goal, but separated by greater periods of time – which to a short-term oriented culture would appear unrelated?

An example of opening the aperture to a greater period of time for monochronic analysis is the topic of nuclear deterrence. The propagation of nuclear weapon capability since 1964 in countries hostile to the United States has diminished the United States' ability to use the threat of nuclear weapons as a deterrent to developing countries in limited war. Technological advances in weapons, communications, banking and a more interdependent world economy have made the world "smaller" and more connected, allowing for change to occur more rapidly and on a larger scale than ever before. Hence, where military victory was once the ultimate goal of conflict, in today's

17

world, a military victory may come to dire consequences in economic and informational terms. The United States was long believed to be the clear victor in a kinetic war with China; the value of American military victory is now very much in doubt. This perspective on a different outcome is based on a 2009 study, which cites Chinese advances in their air force, cyber warfare and their ability to use ballistic missiles to take out American satellites as the key areas where China has made significant capability advancements.[48]

The United States' shortsighted strategic view, typical of a monochronic society, fails to appreciate past American and Chinese lessons. During US-Chinese nuclear negotiations in 1996, when pressured by an American diplomat, People's Liberation Army (PLA) Deputy Chief of Staff Xiong Guangkai recalled the United States threatened the Chinese people with nuclear war three times in the 1950s because the United States had nuclear weapons and the Chinese did not. With China as a nuclear power, Xiong proffered that nuclear threat was useless against China, because the United States "cares more about Los Angeles than Taipei." [49]

Is the defense of Taiwan a vital United States interest? Defending Taiwan may draw the United States into a kinetic war with China; hence determining if this interest is vital requires more thorough analysis. The strategic tension between the United States and China hinges on economic affairs with military issues such as the Taiwan question being ancillary to creating a conflict between the United States and China.

War may appear inevitable between the United States and China given America's history of shortsighted, present-focused strategic application with polychromic cultures. The long-view polychronic Chinese society appears to learn far more from the past than a monchronic time-oriented United States. Misunderstanding and misinterpretation by the United States of Chinese intentions could precipitate conflict more so than the Chinese misinterpreting the United States weak diplomatic short sight. Hence, American strategists must understand Taoist-derived Chinese polychronic time orientation's strategic view. The United States' economic over dependence, sparked by bellicose Chinese information warfare and sustained through insufficient American diplomatic understanding of what the Chinese value may be what precipitates kinetic war between the United States and China.

If understanding time is critical to relating Chinese and American cultures, does time serve as a warfare domain such as land, sea, cyber, air and space? Historically, a warfare domain has been a physical area of military activity. The recognition of cyberspace as a domain added the first non-physical warfare arena. If a domain is defined as a realm in which action occurs and in which we can take action to achieve a desired outcome, time can be considered a domain when framed in the context of understanding Eastern thinking. To the Western military mind, a domain is something geographic or tangible from which, through or into an operation can be conducted.[50] In this definition, time is not a warfare domain – yet. Once time travel or time-differential in operations between opposing forces exists, time is not a warfare domain, but an important factor that requires wide understanding of one's own and adversary's actions and intentions.

Summary

   This paper has laid the groundwork of understanding the concept of time, as well as illustrating the United States and China's time-orientation. The United States has militarily fought Asian foes three times in the 20th Century, the Japanese during World War II, North Korea and Chinese during the Korean War and Vietnamese during the Vietnam War. If the United States and China were to engage in a kinetic war, the United States is no longer the assumed victor. China is a potential United States adversary in the 21st century, and the Chinese will almost certainly be following Sun Tzu's theory of war. The application of this theory of war against the United States is evident in China's economic behavior, potentially rendering the United States military irrelevant, powerless to win a conflict fought on an economic battlefield.

   The United States' strategic reorientation, directing national attention and rigor to the Pacific[51] closely follows the 1967 strategy put forth by then aspiring presidential candidate and geopolitical statesman, Richard Nixon. What has changed in the forty-five years since the future President wrote his article on the rise of Asian power is precisely what was outlined in his paper. Asians want to derive solutions for Asian problems and China wishes to be left to direct and partner the solutions in the Asia-Pacific community of interest. Hence, it is vitally important for Western thinkers and strategists to understand Asian thought and interpret actions of their poloychronic thought process.

   The scientific view of time is widely accepted by Eastern and Western scholars, hence the time space orientation of each nation is largely a cultural difference based on each culture's interpretation of time. This paper explored the applicability of time as a critical factor in the elements of national power, specifically diplomatic, information,

20

military and economic aspects of time. Time is not yet a definable warfare domain, as it cannot be attacked from, into or through to reach an adversary or objective. Just as Einstein's theories must be put to the test for validity, the aspect of time as a potential future domain must periodically be analyzed for relevance.

The United States could embark on a kinetic war with China in response to Chinese economic and cyberspace provocations. China's strategic patience is evident through their long-view dominant economic relationship and bellicose information cyberspace actions toward the United States. The Chinese have yet to illustrate significant military provocation toward the United States. Understanding China's polychronic time orientation and recognizing China's strategic patience will serve US strategists well to sustain a strategy embarked upon over forty-five years ago to continue engagement and dialogue with the Chinese.

Endnotes

[1] Richard M. Nixon, "Asia After Vietnam," Foreign Affairs, Volume 46, Number 1 (1967) http://www.foreignaffairs.com/articles/23927/richard-m-nixon/asia-after-viet-nam (accessed 19 September 2011)

[2] *Ibid.*

[3] Stephen W. Hawking, *A Brief History of Time*, Bantam Press, 1988, New York, New York, Page 17-19.

[4] *Ibid*, p.19.

[5] *Ibid*, p.20.

[6] *Ibid*, p.19.

[7] *Ibid*, p.21.

[8] *Ibid*, p.19.

[9] Stephen Hawking, "How to Build a Time Machine," *Mail Online*, http://www.dailymail.co.uk/home/moslive/article-1269288/STEPHEN-HAWKING-How-build-time-machine.html.

[10] *Ibid.*

[11] "Why is the Concept of Time so Important in Western Culture?" , Quora, Website, http://www.quora.com/why-is-the-concept-of-time-so-important-in-Western-culture accessed 22 January 2012.

[12] Kevin Cunningham, Robert R. Tomes, "Space Time Orientations and Contemporary Political Military Thought", *Armed Forces and Society*, Vol. 31, No. 1, Fall 2004, p 119-140.

[13] Guerrero, L.K., Devito J.A.,& Hecht M.L. (1999). The Nonverbal Communication Reader: Classic and contemporary readings (Second Edition). Long Grove, IL: Waveland Press, Inc., Page 227.

[14] *Ibid*, p.227.

[15] *Ibid*, p.227.

[16] Cohen, R. (2004). Negotiating across cultures: International communication in an interdependent world (rev. ed.). Washington, DC: United States Institute of Peace, Page 36.

[17] Cunningham and Tomes, p119-140.

[18] *Ibid.*

[19] "Linear Versus Circular Logic: Conflict Between Indigenous and Non-Indigenous Logic Systems," 11 June 2006, Website, http://woorama.suite101.com/linear-vs-circular-logic-a2993 accessed 22 January 2012.

[20] Harlan K. Ullman and James P. Wade, "Shock and Awe," 1996, National Defense University of the United States.

[21] "Tao and Taoism 101 Overview: Introduction to Taoism Course," *Personal Tao*, Website, http://personaltao.com/taoism-library/articles/taoism-101/ accessed 22 January 2012.

[22] Francois Jullien, *The Propensity of Things, a History of Efficacy in China* (New York: Zone Books, 1995), Page 27-29

[23] "The Conceptual Scheme of Chinese Philosophical Thinking: Shi – Time," Literati Tradition, website, http://literati-tradition.com/time.html accessed 09 February 2012.

[24] Samuel B. Griffith, *Sun Tzu: The Art of War*, (New York: Oxford University Press, 1963), Foreword.

[25] Mannuel B. Dy, Jr., "The Chinese View of Time: A Passage to Eternity," http://www.crvp.org/book/Series03/III-11/chapter_xx.htm (accessed 19 September 2011)

[26] *Ibid*, p.33.

[27] "Thirty-Six Stratagems, Secret Art of War," *36 Ji,*
http://wengu.tartarie.com/wg/wengu.php?l=36ji (accessed 12 March 2012)

[28] *Ibid.*

[29] Paul B. Farrell, "Secret China War Plan: Trillions in U.S. Debt: Today an Economic Battle; Later, Combat," Marketwatch, http://www.marketwatch.com/story/secret-china-war-plan-trillions-in-us-debt-2011-02-08?pagenumber=1 (accessed 19 September 2011)

[30] "Managing China's transition." David A Adams. United States Naval Institute. Proceedings. Annapolis: Jul 2003. Vol.129, Iss. 7; p. 50

[31] "The 10 Biggest Steel Producing Countries In The World," *Business Insider,*
http://www.businessinsider.com/countries-that-produce-the-most-steel-2011-7#1-china-10 (accessed 19 September 2011)

[32] "IMF Predicts China Will Pass US Economy Sooner than Expected," newsytype.com, http://www.newsytype.com/5690-imf-china-economy-us/ (accessed 19 September 2011)

[33] Gordon G. Chang, "China Threatens to Use Financial Weapon Against America," World Affairs Journal, 09 August 2011, http://www.worldaffairsjournal.org/blog/gordon-g-chang/china-threatens-use-'financial-weapon'-against-america (accessed 10 Feb 2012).

[34] *Ibid.*

[35] *Ibid.*

[36] Farrell

[37] "IMF Predicts China Will Pass US Economy Sooner than Expected," newsytype.com, http://www.newsytype.com/5690-imf-china-economy-us/ (accessed 19 September 2011)

[38] Farrell

[39] Thirty Six Stratagems

[40] "Indian Spatial Concepts," website, http://lewis-clark.org/content/content-article.asp?ArticleID=1263, accessed 12 March 2012

[41] *Ibid.*

[42] *Ibid.*

[43] "Cross Cultural Communications: Beyond Intractability," Website, http://www.beyondintractability.org/node/2565 accessed 09 February 2012.

[44] Anastasia Bibikova and Vadlim Kotelnikov, "Eastern Versus Western Philosophy: Differences and Similarities and World Culture Comparison," Website, http://www.1000ventures.com/business_guide/crosscuttings/cultures_East-West-phylosophy.html accessed 09 February 2012.

[45] Li Mengyu, "The Unique Values of Chinese Traditional Cultural Time Orientation": In Comparison with Western Cultural Time Orientation, University of Louisville Center for Intercultural Communication, Ocean University of China, Website, http://al.comm.louisville.edu/iic/?page_id=342, accessed 09 February 2012.

[46] Thirty Six Stratagems

[47] Thirty Six Stratagems

[48] Farrell

[49] James A. Nathan, Soldiers, Statecraft and History: Coercive Diplomacy and International Order, Westport, CT. Greenwood Publishing Page 119-121

[50] Olen L. Kelley, "Cyberspace Domain: A Warfighting Substantiated Operational Environment Imperative," Strategic Research Project, 2008, United States Army War College, Carlisle, PA

[51] Keith Johnson, "Clinton Says 'Center of Gravity' is Shifting to Asia-Pacific," *Wall Street Journal*, 11 November 2011